COOKIES FOR HOLIDAYS & EVERY DAY

D1159886

NO NONSENSE COOKING GUIDE

COOKIES FOR HOLIDAYS & EVERY DAY

IRENA CHALMERS

LONGMEADOW PRESS

The recipes contained in this book have been tested and tried. However, results may vary depending on the conditions in your kitchen.

COOKIES FOR HOLIDAYS & EVERY DAY

Copyright © 1987 by Irena Chalmers

Published by Longmeadow Press, 201 High Ridge Road, Stamford, Connecticut 06904. No part of this book may be reproduced or used in any form or by any means, electronic or mechanical, including photocopying, recording, or by an information storage and retrieval system, without permission in writing from the publisher.

ISBN 0-681-40273-3

Printed in the United States of America

0 9 8 7 6 5 4 3 2

STAFF FOR NO NONSENSE COOKING GUIDES

EDITORIAL DIRECTION: **Jean Atcheson**

MANAGING EDITOR: **Mary Goodbody**

COVER DESIGN: **Karen Skelton**

ART DIRECTION & DESIGN: **Helene Berinsky**

RECIPE DEVELOPMENT: **Barbara Spiegel**

ASSISTANT EDITORS: **Mary Dauman, Dorothy Atcheson**

PROJECT MANAGER: **Nancy Kipper**

COVER PHOTOGRAPH: **Gerald Zanetti**

TYPESETTING: **ComCom, Allentown, Pennsylvania**

PRODUCTION SERVICES: **William S. Konecky Associates, New York**

CONTENTS

COOKIES

Cookies might be considered our favorite snack. These (usually) rounded little discs of flavor fit nicely into lunchboxes, brown bags, pockets and briefcases; they just as easily sit on the edge of a saucer or dessert plate. One or two cookies satisfy a need for "something sweet," while three or four constitute a generous after-school or after-work snack (particularly with a glass of ice-cold milk).

Supermarket shelves and specialty food shops entice us with all sorts of cookies. Every purveyor claims *that* cookie has the most chocolate chips, the crunchiest nuts, the most peanut butter flavor. Whether the cookies are packaged for long shelf life or baked a few hours before being displayed in a bakery showcase, they are touted as the chewiest, tenderest, most buttery and "old-fashioned" tasting cookies you have ever put in your mouth. And while some commercial products do come within range of meeting these claims—especially those made by the gourmet cookie merchants who have set up shop in malls and on main streets across the land—we all know that the only way a cookie can make claims to greatness is to be home baked.

Here, in this book, are chocolate chip cookies, peanut butter cookies, oatmeal cookies and fudge cookies—to be baked for everyone who knows that a house becomes a home when the cookie jar is filled to the brim with homemade cookies. In these pages you will find crisp and soft cookies, jam filled cookies, ladyfingers, cat's tongues and gingerbread folk. All can be made any time of the year and eaten at any time of the day.

At Christmas, homemade cookies are as important a part of the celebration as the lights on the tree. Long ago, when spices were as precious and as costly as gold, frankincense and myrrh, our ancestors could afford to buy only minute quantities of nutmeg and cinnamon, ginger, aniseed and mace once a year. The spices were baked into cookies that filled the kitchen with rare and exotic fragrances. Today we still follow these traditions, and while we can bake these cookies all year long, we particularly like to do so during the holidays.

When you bake cookies, remember to use only the best ingredients you can find. If you have a choice of fat, always use butter. Not only will the cookies taste better, but the butter forms a firmer dough when it is chilled than margarine or shortening and the cookies will not spread too much in the oven.

We have specified large eggs and all-purpose flour. Unless a recipe indicates that you use brown or confectioners' (powdered) sugar, use granulated. Nuts should be fresh and chopped by hand or in the food processor (be careful not to overgrind the nuts into paste). Store opened containers of nuts in the refrigerator and try to use them within the week while they are still fresh.

Cookies are among the most satisfying sweets to prepare. Children and adults alike respond with smiles and outstretched hands when presented with a plate piled high with just-baked cookies. So, get out the mixer, the baking sheets and the wooden spoons . . . and have fun.

CHAPTER 1

COOKIE JAR COOKIES

These are the cookies of childhood—those big, chewy satisfying cookies that beg to be munched at the kitchen table with a large glass of cold milk. Most keep well and are just right for tucking into lunchboxes or packing in paper bags to take along on car trips.

These cookies are easy to make. All are drop cookies and are quickly prepared with a hand-held or standing electric mixer. Many can be mixed with little effort by hand. This makes them ideal for baking sessions with the kids—they can fill the cookie jar themselves.

BAKING SHEETS: WHICH KIND IS BEST?

Although it really is a matter of personal opinion, the best baking sheets—or cookie sheets as they are also called—do not have a rim. This way the cookies can be lifted off the sheets easily. Heavier baking sheets are preferred, too: they don't warp easily and so remain nice and flat. Their weight also helps keep the cookies from burning.

Peanut Cookies

Makes 3 dozen

Whether you choose to add the chocolate or not, the cookies are mouth-wateringly good—and chocolate fans will agree that the chocolate adds a touch of greatness.

8 tablespoons (4 ounces) butter, softened
1½ cups firmly packed brown sugar
1 large egg
1 teaspoon vanilla extract
1½ cups sifted all-purpose flour
½ teaspoon baking soda
½ teaspoon salt
1 cup finely chopped peanuts
6 ounces semisweet chocolate, chopped (optional)

Beat the butter and sugar in a large bowl until the mixture is light and creamy. Stir in the egg and the vanilla.

Sift together the flour, baking soda and salt. Fold the dry ingredients into the batter. Stir in the peanuts and chill the batter for 1 hour.

Heat the oven to 375 degrees. Lightly butter 2 baking sheets.

Drop the batter onto the baking sheets in teaspoonfuls, about 1½ inches apart. Bake for 8 minutes, until the cookies are lightly browned. Cool on wire racks.

Melt the chopped chocolate in the top of a double boiler over hot water, or in a microwave oven. Drizzle the melted chocolate over the cookies when they have cooled completely.

Coconut Macaroons

Makes 3 dozen

For sweet self-indulgence, try these macaroons with smooth, creamy desserts, or with a piping-hot cup of chocolate or cappuccino.

3 large egg whites
⅛ teaspoon salt
⅛ teaspoon cream of tartar
¾ cup sugar
1 teaspoon vanilla extract
1¼ cups sweetened, flaked coconut
1 tablespoon cornstarch

Heat the oven to 325 degrees. Lightly butter 2 baking sheets.

Put the egg whites, salt and cream of tartar in a bowl and beat until soft peaks form. Beat in the sugar, a tablespoon at a time, until the whites are stiff and shiny. Fold in the vanilla.

Toss the coconut with the cornstarch and fold it into the egg whites.

Drop the mixture onto the baking sheets in teaspoonfuls. Bake for 20 minutes, until the edges are very lightly browned. Cool the cookies on wire racks.

DROP COOKIES

The cookies in this chapter are all drop cookies, which means the batter is dropped from a teaspoon or tablespoon onto cookie sheets. Often the batter is chilled before the cookies are dropped, which helps them keep their shape and cook evenly.

Oatmeal Raisin Cookies

Makes 5 dozen

The classic cookie-jar cookie. These will disappear as fast as you make them.

> *1 cup raisins*
> *12 tablespoons (6 ounces) butter, softened*
> *1 cup packed brown sugar*
> *2 cups sifted flour*
> *½ teaspoon salt*
> *1 teaspoon baking soda*
> *1 teaspoon cinnamon*
> *½ teaspoon allspice*
> *2 large eggs, beaten*
> *¾ cup rolled oats*
> *½ cup chopped pecans or walnuts*

Put the raisins in a bowl, cover them with hot water and set them aside to soak for 5 to 15 minutes, until they are nice and plump. Drain the raisins and pat them dry with paper towels.

Heat the oven to 375 degrees. Lightly butter 2 baking sheets.

Beat the butter and sugar in a large bowl until light and creamy.

Sift together the flour, salt, baking soda and spices. Fold ½ cup of the dry ingredients and half the beaten eggs into the creamed butter. Add the remaining dry ingredients and eggs, folding only until the flour is incorporated. Fold in the raisins, oats and nuts.

Drop the batter onto the baking sheets in teaspoonfuls, about 2 inches apart. Bake for 15 minutes, until the edges are lightly browned. Cool the cookies on wire racks.

Chocolate Chip Cookies

Makes 3 dozen

Everybody's favorite. The orange rind makes this version especially intriguing.

> *8 tablespoons (4 ounces) butter, softened*
> *¼ cup sugar*
> *½ cup packed brown sugar*
> *1 large egg*
> *1¼ cups sifted all-purpose flour*
> *½ teaspoon salt*
> *½ teaspoon baking soda*
> *Grated rind of 1 orange (optional)*
> *¾ cup semisweet chocolate chips*
> *½ cup chopped walnuts*

Heat the oven to 375 degrees. Lightly butter 2 baking sheets.

Beat the butter and both sugars in a large bowl until light and creamy. Add the egg and beat until the mixture is fluffy.

Sift the flour with the salt and baking soda. Add to the creamed butter. Stir in the orange rind, chocolate chips and walnuts.

Drop the batter onto the baking sheets in teaspoonfuls about 2 inches apart. Bake for 10 to 12 minutes, until brown. Cool the cookies on wire racks.

When a recipe calls for brown sugar, you can use either light or dark. The flavor is almost identical and they react similarly in a recipe.

Poppy Seed Cookies

Makes 2 1/2 dozen

The poppy seeds give these cookies a pleasingly crunchy texture.

1/2 cup poppy seeds
1/4 cup hot milk
8 tablespoons (4 ounces) butter, softened
1/2 cup sugar
2 ounces semisweet chocolate, chopped
1 1/2 cups all-purpose flour
1 teaspoon baking powder
1 teaspoon cinnamon
1/2 teaspoon ground cloves
1 cup currants
Grated rind of 1 orange

Poppy seeds have been used in cooking since Biblical times, when they were thought to be a stimulant. Now they appear chiefly as decoration.

Soak the poppy seeds in the milk for 5 minutes or until all the milk is absorbed.

Beat the butter and sugar in a large bowl until the mixture is light and creamy.

Melt the chocolate in the top of a double boiler over hot water, or in a microwave. Stir the melted chocolate into the butter and sugar mixture.

Sift together the flour, baking powder, cinnamon and cloves and fold into the chocolate mixture. Fold in the currants, orange rind and poppy seeds. Chill the batter for 1 hour.

Heat the oven to 350 degrees. Lightly butter 2 baking sheets.

Drop the batter onto the baking sheets by teaspoonfuls, about 1 inch apart. Bake for 15 minutes. Cool the cookies on wire racks.

Raisin Lunchbox Hermits

Makes 2 dozen

Temptingly spicy and chewy, these raisin bars are a treat for anyone's lunchbox, briefcase or brown bag.

> 8 tablespoons (4 ounces) butter, softened
> ¾ cup packed brown sugar
> 1 large egg
> ½ cup molasses
> 1½ cups all-purpose flour
> ½ teaspoon cinnamon
> ½ teaspoon ground nutmeg
> ½ teaspoon ground cloves
> ½ teaspoon baking soda
> ¼ teaspoon salt
> 1½ cups raisins
> ¼ cup chopped walnuts

Heat the oven to 350 degrees. Lightly butter a 9-by-13-by-2-inch baking pan.

Beat the butter and sugar in a large bowl until fluffy. Beat in the egg and then the molasses.

Sift together the flour, spices, baking soda and salt and stir them into the butter mixture. Fold in the raisins and the nuts.

Spread the batter in the pan and bake for 20 to 25 minutes, until the center is still soft but springs back to the touch. Cool completely and then cut into 24 bars. Store the bars in an airtight container.

Old-Fashioned Molasses Cookies

Makes 2½ dozen

The kind grandma used to bake—and the kind you'll be baking for your own grandchildren! The soft, cakelike cookies will keep for a week or more if stored in an airtight container.

> *8 tablespoons (4 ounces) butter, softened*
> *½ cup packed light brown sugar*
> *½ cup light molasses*
> *1 large egg, lightly beaten*
> *2 cups all-purpose flour*
> *2 teaspoons baking soda*
> *½ teaspoon salt*
> *1 teaspoon ground cloves*
> *1 teaspoon powdered ginger*
> *1 teaspoon allspice*
> *¼ cup water*

Heat the oven to 375 degrees. Lightly butter 2 baking sheets.

Combine the butter, brown sugar, molasses and egg in a large bowl and beat until smooth.

Sift together the flour, baking soda, salt and spices. Stir the dry ingredients into the batter, a third at a time, alternating with the water.

Drop the batter onto the baking sheets by tablespoonfuls, about 2 inches apart. Bake for 8 to 10 minutes, or until the cookies are lightly browned and the tops spring back when gently pressed. Cool the cookies on wire racks.

Lemon Wafers

Makes 4 dozen

Be careful to avoid overbaking these crispy-thin, delicately flavored cookies. Wait only a few minutes before transferring them carefully from the baking sheets to wire racks.

> 8 tablespoons (4 ounces) butter, softened
> ½ cup sugar
> 2 large eggs
> 1 teaspoon vanilla extract
> Grated rind of 2 lemons
> 1 teaspoon lemon juice
> 1¼ cups sifted all-purpose flour
> ⅛ teaspoon salt

Beat the butter and sugar in a large bowl until light and creamy.

Stir in the eggs, vanilla, lemon rind and juice. Fold in the flour and the salt. Chill the batter for 1 hour. (This will prevent it from spreading too much during baking.)

Heat the oven to 350 degrees. Lightly butter 2 baking sheets.

Drop the batter onto the baking sheets in teaspoonfuls about 1½ inches apart. Bake for 6 to 7 minutes, until the edges are very lightly browned. Take the cookies from the oven and let them cool on the baking sheets for 2 to 3 minutes. Carefully transfer them with a metal spatula to wire racks to cool completely.

For best results, always squeeze fresh lemons for lemon juice—after you have grated any rind you need.

CHAPTER 2

REFRIGERATOR COOKIES

If you are frantically busy (and who isn't?) but love home-baked cookies so much you cannot do without them (and who can?), these are the cookies for you. They used to be called icebox cookies, and the principle hasn't changed since refrigerators replaced the old-fashioned block of ice in a wooden chest. The dough can be whipped together several days in advance of baking and left in the refrigerator until *you* are ready for it. Or, if you really like to plan ahead, you can freeze the dough for months, wrapped in an additional coat of freezer paper or heavy-duty aluminum foil. Then, when the urge strikes for something hot from the oven, you can have cookies in minutes.

The usual practice is to form the dough for these cookies into cylinders about two inches in diameter; once these have been chilled, they can easily be sliced into rounds, as thick or thin as you please. In appearance and texture, the cookies are very similar to the cookies you roll out with a rolling pin, but because the dough is firmed up in the refrigerator, it generally requires slightly less flour than the dough for rolled cookies. Consequently, refrigerator cookies tend to taste a little more buttery.

Sugar Cookies

Makes 4 dozen

The traditional crunchy, sweet sugar cookie is just about as American—and as popular—as apple pie.

> 8 tablespoons (4 ounces) butter, softened
> 1 cup sugar
> 2 large eggs
> 2 tablespoons milk
> 1 teaspoon vanilla extract
> Grated rind of 1 lemon
> 2½ cups sifted all-purpose flour
> 1½ teaspoons baking powder
> ¼ teaspoon salt
> 2 tablespoons superfine sugar

Beat the butter and 1 cup of sugar in a large bowl until light and creamy.

In a separate bowl, combine the eggs, milk, vanilla and lemon rind.

Sift together the flour, baking powder and salt.

Gradually add the egg-milk mixture to the creamed butter, alternating with the sifted dry ingredients. Blend well after each addition.

Divide the dough into 4 pieces and put each on a large piece of wax paper or aluminum foil. Shape the dough into cylinders about 2 inches thick. Wrap each cylinder well and chill for 2 hours, or until very firm.

Heat the oven to 375 degrees. Lightly butter 2 baking sheets.

Cut the dough cylinders into slices about ¼ inch thick and put them on the baking sheets about 1 inch apart. Bake for 10 minutes, until the cookies are very lightly browned.

Sprinkle the cookies with superfine sugar and cool on wire racks.

Take frozen dough from the freezer the day before you plan to bake and let it thaw gradually in the refrigerator until it is the proper handling consistency; then proceed with the recipe.

Vanilla and Chocolate Pinwheels

Makes about 6 dozen

In spite of their intricate pattern, these pretty, two-tone cookies are a snap to make.

LIGHT DOUGH:
8 tablespoons (4 ounces) butter, softened
¼ cup sugar
1 teaspoon vanilla extract
1 large egg
2 cups all-purpose flour
¼ teaspoon baking powder

DARK DOUGH:
8 tablespoons (4 ounces) butter, softened
¼ cup sugar
1 teaspoon vanilla extract
2 cups less 2 tablespoons all-purpose flour
3 tablespoons unsweetened cocoa powder
¼ teaspoon baking powder

To make the light dough, combine the butter, sugar and vanilla in a large bowl and beat until light and creamy. Beat in the egg.

Sift together the dry ingredients and stir into the batter to make a smooth, soft dough.

Prepare the dark dough in the same way.

Put each piece of dough between 2 sheets of wax paper. Use a rolling pin to roll each one into an 8-by-15-inch rectangle. Chill the rectangles for 30 minutes, until firm.

Peel the top sheet of paper from each rectangle. Invert the dark layer over the light layer and peel off the paper. Carefully invert the dough and peel off the last piece of paper.

Trim the edges of the rectangle and then roll the dough into a cylinder, starting from one of the long edges of the rectangle and rolling lengthwise as if it were a jelly roll. Wrap the rolled dough in wax paper or a clean dry dish towel and chill for 30 minutes.

Heat the oven to 350 degrees. Lightly butter 2 baking sheets.

Cut the dough cylinder into thin slices, barely ¼ inch thick, and put them on the baking sheets about 1 inch apart. Bake for 7 to 10 minutes. Cool the cookies on wire racks.

ALL SUGAR IS SWEET

All the recipes in this book were developed using granulated white sugar—the kind everybody buys in the super-market—unless they specifically call for other kinds such as confectioners' (powdered), light or dark brown sugar or granulated brown sugar. If you substitute one kind of sugar for another this will affect both the flavor and texture of the cookies, so try to avoid it if possible. (You *could,* of course, come up with a delightful new variation, but you are more likely to have to dispose of the results than display them!)

Superfine sugar is finely ground granulated white sugar. It is widely available but if you do not have any on hand, simply grind some granulated sugar in a blender.

When using brown sugar, be sure to pack it firmly when you measure it. If the sugar has hardened into a solid block—as it is apt to do after it is opened and absorbs moisture—you can soften it in a very low oven or by putting it in a microwave for a few minutes.

Icebox Spice Cookies

Makes 5 dozen

"Sugar and spice and all things nice"—that's what these cookies are made of.

12 tablespoons (6 ounces) butter, softened
1½ cups packed dark brown sugar
1 large egg
1 teaspoon vanilla extract
3 cups sifted all-purpose flour
2 teaspoons baking powder
1 teaspoon cinnamon
¼ teaspoon salt
½ teaspoon ground nutmeg or allspice

Allspice is so called because its taste seems to blend cloves, cinnamon and nutmeg. It is usually sold already ground, while nutmeg tastes much better when you grate it yourself using a fine grater.

Beat the butter in a large bowl until it is creamy. Add the sugar and beat until the mixture is light and fluffy. Beat in the egg and the vanilla.

Sift together the flour, baking powder, cinnamon, salt and nutmeg or allspice. Gradually fold the sifted dry ingredients into the batter, mixing well after each addition.

Divide the dough into thirds and shape each portion into a cylinder about 2 inches thick. Wrap each cylinder in wax paper or transparent wrap and chill for several hours.

Heat the oven to 375 degrees.

Using a sharp, heavy knife, cut the dough into slices about ¼ inch thick. Put the slices on unbuttered baking sheets, about 2 inches apart. Bake for 10 to 12 minutes. Cool the cookies on wire racks.

Fruit Cookies

Makes 3 1/2 dozen

Currants or raisins, figs or apricots—the choice is yours for these flavorful, chewy cookies. Mix the dried fruit with a tablespoon or two of the measured flour before you chop it. This stops the fruit from sticking together and makes the job easier.

> *8 tablespoons (4 ounces) butter, softened*
> *1 cup sugar*
> *1 large egg*
> *½ teaspoon vanilla extract*
> *2 cups sifted all-purpose flour*
> *1 teaspoon baking powder*
> *⅛ teaspoon salt*
> *½ cup raisins or currants*
> *½ cup finely chopped dried figs or apricots*

Beat the butter in a large bowl until it is light and creamy. Add the sugar and continue beating until the mixture is fluffy. Beat in the egg and vanilla.

Sift together the flour, baking powder and salt and fold into the creamed mixture. Mix well and stir in the fruit.

Shape the dough into a cylinder about 12 inches long. Wrap in transparent wrap and chill for several hours or overnight.

Heat the oven to 375 degrees.

Using a sharp, heavy knife, cut the dough into ¼-inch-thick slices. Set them about 2 inches apart on unbuttered baking sheets and bake for 10 to 12 minutes, until lightly browned. Cool the cookies on wire racks.

Coconut Washboards

Makes 4 dozen

An old-fashioned sort of cookie, as befits its name, which comes from the ridges you make in it with a fork before baking. It has a pleasant, soft texture.

8 tablespoons (4 ounces) butter, softened
1 teaspoon vanilla extract
¾ cup packed light brown sugar
1 large egg
2 tablespoons water
2 cups all-purpose flour
¾ teaspoon baking powder
¼ teaspoon baking soda
1 cup firmly packed sweetened shredded coconut

Beat the butter in a large bowl until smooth and creamy. Add the vanilla and the brown sugar and continue to beat until the mixture is smooth. Beat in the egg and the water.

Sift together the flour, baking powder and baking soda. Gradually add the sifted ingredients to the butter mixture, mixing well after each addition. Stir in the coconut.

Drop the dough by large spoonfuls onto 2 sheets of wax paper. Form each portion of dough into a cylinder, each about 8 inches long, 2½ inches wide and 1 inch high. Wrap well and chill for several hours.

Heat the oven to 375 degrees.

Using a sharp, heavy knife, cut the dough into ¼-inch-thick slices and put on unbuttered baking sheets about 2 inches apart. Dip a fork in flour and press the tines lightly onto the tops of the cookies to form "washboard" ridges.

Bake the cookies for about 10 minutes until lightly browned. Cool on wire racks.

Peanut Butter and Honey Slices

Makes about 6 dozen

Peanut butter and honey make a winning combination.
Use creamy, not crunchy, peanut butter, please!

> 5 tablespoons (2½ ounces) butter, softened
> ½ cup sugar
> ½ cup honey
> 1 cup creamy peanut butter
> 1 large egg
> 2 cups sifted all-purpose flour
> 1 teaspoon baking powder
> ½ teaspoon baking soda
> ¼ teaspoon salt

Beat the butter in a large bowl until smooth. Add the
sugar, honey, peanut butter and egg and beat until well
combined.

Sift together the flour, baking powder and salt and
stir into the peanut butter mixture.

Divide the dough in half. Set each portion on wax
paper and shape into flattened rolls about 10 inches
long, 2½ inches wide and 1½ inches high. Wrap well
and chill for several hours, or up to 3 days.

Heat the oven to 400 degrees. Lightly butter 2 baking
sheets.

Remove the dough from the refrigerator, and cut
into ¼-inch-thick slices, using a sharp, heavy knife. Put
the slices on the baking sheets and bake for 8 to 10
minutes, until the cookies are an even, light brown
color. Cool the cookies on wire racks.

CHAPTER 3

ROLLED AND HAND-FORMED COOKIES

Now you are really going to have fun! Making rolled and hand-formed cookies is one of the real pleasures of the kitchen. It is true that they take a little more time and equipment than other kinds of cookies, but don't let this stop you. Just choose a day when you feel at ease and unrushed, and ready to enjoy yourself.

A recipe may suggest that you cut the cookies out with a round biscuit cutter, but if you prefer you can use your favorite cookie cutters instead. Keep an eye out for old-time cookie cutters, which are frequently sold in antique shops, at tag sales and flea markets. They tend to be more whimsical than modern ones and are fun to collect.

When you roll the cookies, be sure to flour the work surface and rolling pin *lightly.* Too much flour worked into the dough during rolling will toughen it. Chilling the dough, as suggested in these recipes, makes it easier to handle and less sticky than room-temperature dough. Don't handle the dough more than necessary—though you might want to break off a good-sized chunk to give to a young helper to shape while you cut out the rest of the cookies.

Spice Cookies with Brandy

Makes 4 dozen

Serve these cookies on brisk fall afternoons with hot spiced apple cider—if you like, you can add a drop or two of brandy to the cider, as well.

1 cup (8 ounces) butter, softened
¾ cup granulated sugar
¾ cup packed dark brown sugar
2 large eggs, beaten
2 tablespoons brandy
3½ cups sifted all-purpose flour
¼ teaspoon salt
½ teaspoon baking powder
1½ teaspoons cinnamon
½ teaspoon ground nutmeg
½ teaspoon mace

Beat the butter with both the sugars in a large bowl until the mixture is light and creamy. Stir in the eggs and the brandy.

Sift together the flour, salt, baking powder and spices. Fold them into the creamed butter mixture. Shape the dough into a ball and chill for 1 hour.

Heat the oven to 325 degrees. Lightly butter 2 baking sheets.

Cut the chilled dough in half. Return one half to the refrigerator until you are ready to use it. Set the other half on a floured work surface and roll it out as thin as possible with a lightly floured rolling pin. Stamp out 2- or 2½-inch cookies with a cookie cutter or an inverted glass. Put the cookies on the prepared sheets.

Bake for about 8 minutes. Let the cookies cool on the baking sheets for a few minutes before transferring them to wire racks to cool completely. Repeat the procedure with the remaining dough.

If you are trying to roll dough very thin, rolling it out on a lightly floured pastry cloth helps keep the dough from sticking.

Pecan Delights

Makes 3 dozen

When the pecan sack is empty, try making these little cookies with walnuts, almonds or filberts.

1 cup (8 ounces) butter, softened
¾ cup sugar
3 large eggs, separated
1 teaspoon vanilla extract
Grated rind of 1 orange
2 cups sifted all-purpose flour
⅛ teaspoon salt
1 cup ground pecans

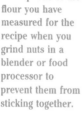

Add about 2 tablespoons of the flour you have measured for the recipe when you grind nuts in a blender or food processor to prevent them from sticking together.

Beat the butter and sugar in a large bowl until light and creamy. Stir in the egg yolks, vanilla and orange rind. Set the egg whites aside for later use.

Fold the flour and salt into the mixture and chill for 1 hour.

Heat the oven to 375 degrees. Lightly butter 2 cookie sheets.

Beat the egg whites just until frothy. Put the ground nuts in a shallow dish or on a plate.

Break off small pieces of dough and shape them into ½-inch balls. Dip the balls in the egg whites and then roll them in the ground nuts. Put them on the baking sheets and bake for 10 minutes, or until they are lightly browned. Transfer the cookies to wire racks to cool. Repeat the procedure with the remaining dough.

Molasses Crisps

Makes 5 dozen

As their name promises, these are crispy, crunchy cookies with the deep, dark flavor of molasses.

> *8 tablespoons (4 ounces) butter, softened*
> *¼ cup packed brown sugar*
> *¾ cup molasses*
> *Grated rind of 1 orange*
> *3 cups sifted all-purpose flour*
> *½ teaspoon salt*
> *½ teaspoon baking soda*
> *1 teaspoon powdered ginger*
> *½ teaspoon ground cloves*
> *1 teaspoon cinnamon*

Beat the butter with the sugar in a large bowl until the mixture is light and creamy. Stir in the molasses and orange rind.

Sift together the remaining ingredients and fold them into the butter mixture. Shape the dough into a ball and chill for 1 hour.

Heat the oven to 375 degrees. Lightly butter 2 cookie sheets.

Cut the chilled dough in half and put one half back in the refrigerator. Set the other half on a floured work surface and roll it out with a lightly floured rolling pin until the dough is very thin. Stamp out 2- or 3-inch cookies with a cookie cutter or an inverted glass. Put the cookies on the prepared baking sheets.

Bake for 6 minutes, or until the edges turn light brown. Let the cookies cool on the baking sheets for a few minutes until they are firm enough to lift without breaking. Transfer them to wire racks to cool completely. Repeat the procedure with the remaining dough.

Sour Cream Walnut Cookies

Makes 2 dozen

Cloves, walnuts and the tang of sour cream make these cookies just right during the Christmas holidays—or any time of year! Serve them with a tall glass of lemonade or iced tea.

> *8 tablespoons (4 ounces) butter, softened*
> *¼ cup sugar*
> *1 large egg yolk*
> *½ cup sour cream*
> *1½ cups sifted all-purpose flour*
> *½ teaspoon baking soda*
> *½ teaspoon ground cloves*
> *½ cup ground walnuts*
> *Grated rind of 1 orange*

Beat the butter and sugar in a large bowl until the mixture is light and creamy. Stir in the egg yolk and the sour cream.

Sift the flour with the baking soda and cloves and fold into the butter mixture. Stir in the nuts and the orange rind. Shape the dough into a ball and chill for 1 hour.

Heat the oven to 325 degrees. Lightly butter 2 baking sheets.

Break off small pieces of the dough and roll them into 1-inch balls. Put them on the baking sheets and flatten them with a fork.

Bake for 10 minutes, or until the edges are lightly browned. Transfer the cookies to wire racks to cool. Repeat the procedure with the remaining dough.

Sesame Seed Cookies

Makes 3 dozen

You can buy small jars of sesame seeds in most supermarkets. They are sold in larger quantities in shops specializing in Chinese, Japanese and Middle Eastern foods and it is more economical to buy them this way if you plan to use them often.

1 cup sesame seeds
½ cup sweetened, flaked coconut
8 tablespoons (4 ounces) butter, softened
1 cup packed brown sugar
1 large egg
2 teaspoons vanilla extract
Grated rind of 1 lemon
2 cups sifted all-purpose flour
½ teaspoon baking soda
1 teaspoon baking powder
⅛ teaspoon salt

Heat the oven to 350 degrees. Lightly butter 2 baking sheets.

Spread the sesame seeds and coconut on an unbuttered baking sheet and toast in the oven for 8 minutes, stirring once or twice. Remove them from the oven, stir again, and set aside to cool.

Beat the butter and sugar in a large bowl until the mixture is light and creamy. Stir in the egg, vanilla, lemon rind, sesame seeds and coconut.

Sift together the flour, baking soda, baking powder and salt. Fold into the butter mixture.

Pinch off small pieces of dough and shape them into ½-inch balls. Set them on the buttered baking sheets and bake for 10 minutes until lightly browned. Cool the cookies on wire racks. Repeat the procedure with the remaining dough.

Sesame seeds will keep well for a month or two in a closed bag or box in a dry, cool place—*not* the refrigerator.

Hazelnut Crescents

Makes 2 dozen

Crunchy, new-moon-shaped teatime treats.

6 tablespoons (3 ounces) butter, softened
⅓ cup sugar
1 cup plus 2 tablespoons all-purpose flour
¾ cup finely chopped toasted hazelnuts
1 large egg, beaten

To toast hazelnuts, simply spread on a baking tray and bake in a 350-degree oven for 5 to 7 minutes.

Beat the butter and sugar in a large bowl until creamy. Stir in the flour, then the nuts and mix well.

Stir in 1 tablespoon of the beaten egg and knead lightly until the dough holds together.

Heat the oven to 350 degrees. Lightly butter 2 cookie sheets.

Set the dough on a lightly floured work surface and roll it out to a thickness of about ¼ inch. Stamp out the dough, using a 2-to-3-inch crescent cookie cutter. Put the cookies on the baking sheets and brush with the remaining egg.

Bake for about 8 minutes, until the edges are lightly browned. Transfer the cookies to wire racks to cool. Repeat the procedure with the remaining dough.

WOODEN COOKIE MOLDS: AN OLD-FASHIONED ART

Begin by lightly oiling the mold. Next, break off pieces of chilled dough and shape them into walnut-sized balls. Press the balls into the mold. Use a kitchen knife to level off the dough and then trim the edges. Gently tap the molded cookies out onto the prepared baking sheets and bake as instructed in the recipe.

Speculaas

Makes 3 dozen

Here is an old Dutch recipe for cookies that were baked in decorative wooden molds carved to resemble people, flowers and animals. Charming reproductions of the folk-art molds are sold in many kitchenware shops and you can sometimes find older versions in antique stores—and, of course, you can also shape the dough with any cookie cutters of your own choosing.

> *4 tablespoons (2 ounces) butter, softened*
> *½ cup packed light brown sugar*
> *1 large egg, separated*
> *1 cup sifted all-purpose flour*
> *⅛ teaspoon salt*
> *¼ teaspoon ground nutmeg*
> *1 teaspoon cinnamon*
> *¼ teaspoon mace*
> *¼ teaspoon white pepper*

Beat the butter with the sugar in a large bowl until the mixture is light and creamy. Stir in the egg yolk.

Sift together the dry ingredients and fold them into the butter mixture. Chill the dough for at least 1 hour.

Heat the oven to 350 degrees. Lightly butter 2 baking sheets.

Put the chilled dough on a floured work surface and roll it out to a thickness of about ¼ inch using a lightly floured rolling pin. Cut into shapes with cookie cutters and put the cookies on the prepared baking sheets. Beat the egg white until frothy and brush it onto the cookies.

Bake for 15 minutes. Transfer the cookies to wire racks to cool. Repeat the procedure with the remaining dough.

Ginger Crackles

Makes about 4 dozen

Butter is usually the preferred fat for cookies, but these crackly ginger cookies seem to taste just as good made with vegetable shortening—good news for anyone on a special diet.

> *2 cups sifted all-purpose flour*
> *1 tablespoon powdered ginger*
> *2 teaspoons baking soda*
> *1 teaspoon cinnamon*
> *½ teaspoon salt*
> *12 tablespoons (6 ounces) butter or solid vegetable shortening*
> *1 cup sugar*
> *1 large egg*
> *¼ cup molasses*
> *Sugar, for rolling*

Heat the oven to 350 degrees. Lightly grease 2 baking sheets.

Sift the flour, ginger, baking soda, cinnamon and salt together twice.

Combine the butter or shortening with the sugar in a large bowl and beat until the mixture is soft and light. Beat in the egg and the molasses.

Add the sifted dry ingredients to the butter mixture, a third at a time, mixing well until a smooth dough has formed.

Lightly flour your hands. Break off pieces of the dough and shape them into 1-inch balls. Roll each ball in sugar and set them on the baking sheets about 2 inches apart.

Bake the cookies for 15 minutes, until lightly browned. Cool on wire racks. Repeat the procedure with the remaining dough.

Almond Squares

Makes 4 dozen

After you roll the chilled dough out into a rectangle, you simply cut it into squares for baking. Different shapes—rectangles, ovals or circles, for instance—taste equally delicious.

> 1½ cups all-purpose flour
> ½ cup ground almonds
> ⅓ cup sugar
> 8 tablespoons (4 ounces) butter, chilled and cut into pieces
> 1 large egg, lightly beaten
> 1 large egg white, lightly beaten
> Sugar, for sprinkling
> 48 blanched almond halves

Combine the flour, ground almonds and sugar in a large bowl. Add the butter and work it in with your fingertips until the mixture resembles coarse crumbs.

Add the egg and mix with your hands to form a cohesive dough. Chill the dough for at least 30 minutes, until firm.

Heat the oven to 325 degrees. Lightly butter 2 cookie sheets.

Put the dough between 2 sheets of wax paper and roll it into a rectangle about ¼ inch thick. Peel off the top sheet of paper. Brush the dough with the beaten egg white. Sprinkle with sugar and cut into 1-inch squares with a sharp knife.

Put the squares on the baking sheets, about 1 inch apart. Lightly press an almond half into the center of each square. Bake for 12 to 15 minutes and cool on wire racks. Repeat the procedure with the remaining dough.

CHAPTER 4

FILLED COOKIES

Who can resist a cookie generously filled with a sweet cream or fruit preserve? Homemade filled cookies are treats to make for special occasions or simply for days when you are in the mood to do something extra nice for your family.

Many of the cookies in this chapter are rolled and shaped before they are filled, so you may want to read the introduction to the previous chapter on Rolled and Hand-Formed Cookies before you begin.

Fudge and Almond Purses

Makes 2½ dozen

These tiny packages are just bursting with a chocolate-almond filling that really *does* melt in your mouth.

FILLING:
4 tablespoons (2 ounces) butter, softened
½ cup sugar

1 large egg yolk
½ teaspoon vanilla extract
½ teaspoon almond extract
¼ cup unsweetened cocoa powder
½ cup finely chopped almonds

DOUGH:
1½ cups all-purpose flour
¼ teaspoon salt
8 tablespoons (4 ounces) butter
3 tablespoons cold water
1½ teaspoons vanilla extract
½ teaspoon almond extract
Confectioners' sugar, for sprinkling
Flour, for sprinkling

Heat the oven to 350 degrees. Lightly butter 2 baking sheets.

To make the filling, combine the butter, sugar, egg yolk, vanilla and almond extracts in a bowl and beat well to blend. Stir in the cocoa and the nuts and mix well.

To make the dough, stir together the flour and the salt. Add the butter and work it in with your fingertips, a fork or a pastry blender until the mixture resembles coarse crumbs. Add the water and the vanilla and almond extracts and mix well. The dough will be sticky.

Generously sprinkle a pastry cloth or work surface with a mixture of confectioners' sugar and flour. Divide the dough in half and roll out one half as thin as possible, using a lightly floured rolling pin. Cut into 2½-inch squares. Repeat with the remaining dough. Place the squares on the baking sheets.

Drop 1 level teaspoon of the filling onto the center of each square. Bring the four corners together and pinch to seal. Bake for 15 to 20 minutes, until the tops are lightly browned.

Apricot Cream Cheese Cookies

Makes 2½ dozen

For especially tender cookies, try these ones made from a light cream cheese pastry and filled with apricot preserves. If you like raspberry or strawberry preserves, use them instead of apricot.

1 cup all-purpose flour
8 tablespoons (4 ounces) butter, softened
4 ounces cream cheese
⅓ cup apricot preserves
1 large egg white
Sugar, for dusting

Sift the flour into a large bowl. Add the butter and cheese and work them into the flour with your fingertips or a pastry blender until the mixture resembles coarse crumbs. Go on working the dough with your hands until it forms a ball. Chill the dough for about 1 hour.

Heat the oven to 375 degrees.

Roll out the dough on a lightly floured work surface until it is very thin. Cut it into 3-by-2-inch rectangles. Spread each rectangle with a scant teaspoon of preserves, leaving a ½-inch border.

Roll up the rectangles to form 3-inch-long cylinders. Pinch the ends to seal. Put the rolls on unbuttered baking sheets, seam side down. Gently tuck the sealed ends under.

Beat the egg white until it is slightly frothy. Brush it over the rolls and dust them with sugar. Bake for 15 minutes, or until golden. Cool the cookies on wire racks. Fill and bake the remaining dough.

Raspberry Sandwich Cookies

Makes 20 to 40 cookies

> 1 cup (8 ounces) butter, softened
> ¼ cup sugar
> 2 large egg yolks
> 2 teaspoons vanilla extract
> Grated rind of 1 lemon
> 2½ cups sifted all-purpose flour
> ⅛ teaspoon salt
> ½ cup raspberry preserves
>
> FROSTING:
> 2 tablespoons lemon juice
> 1 cup confectioners' sugar
> Cold water

Beat the butter with the sugar in a large bowl until the mixture is light and creamy. Stir in the egg yolks, vanilla and lemon rind.

Combine the flour and salt and fold them into the butter mixture. Shape the dough into a ball, cover with transparent wrap and chill for at least 1 hour.

Heat the oven to 350 degrees. Lightly butter 2 baking sheets.

Cut the chilled dough into 4 pieces and roll out each one in turn to a ¼-inch thickness. Stamp out circles with a cookie cutter or inverted glass and put them on the baking sheets. Bake for 10 minutes, until lightly browned. Transfer to wire racks to cool. Repeat the procedure with the remaining dough.

When the circles are cold, spread half of them with the preserves and top with the remainder.

To make the frosting, stir the lemon juice into the confectioners' sugar. Add just enough cold water to give the mixture a medium-thin consistency. Spread a little over the top of each cookie sandwich.

How many cookies? For 40, make circles about 1 1/2 inches in diameter; for 20, about 3 1/2 inches.

Apple and Nut Pockets

Makes 2 dozen

A generous sprinkling of confectioners' sugar leaves these filled cookie "pockets" snowy white. Make the cookie dough a day ahead of time for the best flavor.

DOUGH:

8 tablespoons (4 ounces) butter, softened
1¼ cups sugar
1½ teaspoons vanilla extract
1 large egg
2½ cups sifted all-purpose flour
¼ teaspoon baking soda
½ teaspoon salt

FILLING:

2 cups apple butter
3 tablespoons lemon juice
1 tablespoon grated lemon peel
⅓ cup finely chopped walnuts
⅓ cup finely chopped pecans
Confectioners' sugar, for dusting

To make the dough, beat the butter until it is light. Add the sugar and the vanilla extract and beat until the mixture is fluffy. Beat in the egg.

Sift the flour with the baking powder and the salt. Gradually add the dry ingredients to the butter mixture, beating well after each addition. Wrap the dough in transparent wrap and chill overnight.

To make the filling, combine all the ingredients in a bowl and mix well. Cover with transparent wrap and chill until you are ready to bake the cookies.

Heat the oven to 400 degrees.

Divide the dough into 4 portions. Working with one portion at a time, roll the dough out on a lightly floured work surface to a thickness of ⅛ inch, using a lightly floured rolling pin. Stamp out rounds with a 3-inch cookie cutter.

Set the rounds on 2 unbuttered baking sheets, ½ inch apart. Place a rounded teaspoonful of the filling in the center of each.

Roll and stamp out a second portion of dough in the same way and place the rounds on top of the filled cookies. Dust your fingers with flour and seal the edges of the cookies together. Recut them to neaten the edges, using a slightly smaller cookie cutter. Do not worry if cracks appear in the surface.

Bake the cookies for 12 to 15 minutes, or until they are lightly browned. Cool on wire racks and sprinkle with confectioners' sugar. Bake the remaining dough and filling in the same way.

FRUIT BUTTERS

Fruit butters are dense, delicious concentrations of fruit and flavor. Despite the name, they contain no dairy products and are made wholly from fruit (often with a little sugar and spices added).

You can easily make your own fruit butters by cooking fruit, such as apples or peaches, slowly into a thick sauce. Strain the pulp, flavor it to taste with sugar and spices, and continue cooking over very low heat until nearly all the moisture has evaporated and the mixture has the consistency of butter.

Almond Meringue Horns

Makes 3 dozen

In these delicate crescent cookies, subtly flavored with almonds, the meringue is used as the filling instead of the more usual outside casing.

DOUGH:
2 cups all-purpose flour
¼ teaspoon salt
8 tablespoons (4 ounces) butter, cut into small
    pieces
1½ teaspoons (½ package) active dry yeast
2 tablespoons warm water
2 large egg yolks
¼ cup sour cream
1 teaspoon vanilla extract

FILLING:
2 large egg whites
½ cup superfine sugar
¼ teaspoon almond extract
1 cup finely chopped blanched almonds
Confectioners' sugar, for dusting

Stir together the flour and salt. Add the butter and work it in with your fingertips or a pastry blender until the mixture resembles coarse crumbs.

Sprinkle the yeast into the warm water and stir to dissolve. Stir the egg yolks, sour cream and vanilla into the yeast. Gradually add the liquid to the flour mixture, mixing until the dough forms a ball. Cover and chill for at least 1 hour, until the dough is firm enough to roll.

To make the filling, beat the egg whites until they form very soft peaks. Add the sugar and almond extract and continue to beat until stiff peaks form. Fold in the nuts.

Heat the oven to 375 degrees. Lightly butter 2 baking sheets.

Roll out the dough on a lightly floured work surface until it is very thin. Cut it into triangles about 2 inches wide at the base and 3 inches high. Spread the meringue filling on the triangles and roll them up, starting at the base. Gently curve the rolls into crescent shapes and put them on the prepared baking sheets.

Bake the cookies for 12 to 15 minutes, until they are lightly browned. Transfer them to wire racks to cool. Roll out the remaining dough and fill and bake in the same way.

When all the cookies are completely cooled, dust with confectioners' sugar.

MAD ABOUT MERINGUE

How can sweetened egg whites become so delectable simply by being beaten to snow-white stiff peaks and dried in the oven? Meringues are one of the showiest and easiest of confections.

Some tips: Never try to make meringues on a rainy day. The sugar in the meringue will attract moisture and leave the confection sticky and chewy. Before you begin beating the egg whites, be sure you have a perfectly clean, dry bowl and that the beaters are dry as well. Take care that no fat (which includes egg yolk) gets into the whites.

And it is true: a copper bowl is best for beating egg whites. They rise to—and maintain—fantastic heights.

Cookie Jewels

These gems have brilliant red and green centers. Try other clear, brightly colored jellies, too—apple, apricot or blueberry, for example.

> *8 tablespoons (4 ounces) butter, softened*
> *¼ cup packed light brown sugar*
> *1 large egg, separated*
> *1 cup all-purpose flour*
> *⅛ teaspoon salt*
> *½ cup ground walnuts*
> *¼ cup red currant jelly*
> *¼ cup mint jelly*

Beat the butter and sugar in a large bowl until the mixture is light and fluffy. Stir in the egg yolk.

Add the flour and salt and mix well. Chill the batter for at least 15 minutes, until it is firm enough to handle.

Heat the oven to 300 degrees. Lightly butter 2 cookie sheets.

Beat the egg white in a small bowl until frothy. Lightly flour your hands. Break off small pieces of dough and roll them into flattened balls, about the size of a quarter. Dip them in the beaten egg white and roll in the ground walnuts.

Set the cookies on the baking sheets about 1 inch apart. Lightly press the centers with your thumb or a thimble to make a shallow well in each. Bake the cookies for 15 minutes, then press the well down again. Bake for 10 minutes more. Cool the cookies on wire racks.

When the cookies are still slightly warm, fill half of them with the red currant jelly and the other half with the mint jelly.

CHAPTER 5

CHOCOLATE COOKIES

Chances are, this is the first chapter you turned to when you opened this book. And why not? Chocolate is a favorite with almost everyone. Its dark, deep deliciousness tempts even the most hardened dessert-hater, the most avid dieter and the most fervent sugar-avoider. Baked into cookies such as the ones in this chapter, it is more seductive than ever.

All kinds of chocolate are used in these recipes, from cocoa to semisweet. Cocoa powder is easy to bake with as it can be mixed with the other dry ingredients and then incorporated into the batter. But it lacks some of the intense chocolaty flavor that block chocolate has so abundantly. Unsweetened and semisweet chocolate should be chopped and melted before being mixed with the other ingredients. Unsweetened chocolate is sometimes called baking chocolate and sometimes just plain chocolate. As you would expect, bittersweet chocolate is less sweet than semisweet, but you may interchange them freely in these recipes.

Fudge Cookies

Makes 3 dozen

8 tablespoons (4 ounces) butter, softened
1¼ cups packed brown sugar
2 large eggs
¼ cup unsweetened cocoa powder
1½ cups sifted all-purpose flour
½ teaspoon baking soda
¼ teaspoon salt
1 teaspoon vanilla extract
½ cup chopped nuts

Beat the butter and sugar until the mixture is light and creamy. Add the eggs, one at a time, beating well after each addition.

Sift together the cocoa, flour, baking soda and salt and fold into the butter mixture. Stir in the vanilla and fold in the nuts. Chill the mixture for 1 hour.

Heat the oven to 350 degrees. Lightly butter 2 cookie sheets.

Drop the batter onto the baking sheets in teaspoonfuls, 1½ inches apart, and bake for 10 minutes. Remove the cookies from the sheets while they are still warm and cool them on wire racks. Bake the remaining batter in the same way.

THE WHITE CHOCOLATE REVOLUTION

Essentially, white chocolate is a mixture of sugar, cocoa butter and milk solids. It contains no chocolate liquor, the element in the cocoa bean that makes other chocolates brown and taste distinctively of "chocolate." Read the label carefully when buying white chocolate to be sure you do not confuse it with "summer" or "confectionery" coatings which contain hardened vegetable fats instead of pure cocoa butter.

White Chocolate Chunk Cookies with Macadamia Nuts

Makes 6 dozen

The combination of sweet white chocolate and buttery macadamia nuts has become a new American classic.

8 tablespoons (4 ounces) butter, softened
1 cup packed light brown sugar
½ cup granulated sugar
2 large eggs
2 tablespoons unsweetened cocoa powder
1 teaspoon vanilla extract
2 cups all-purpose flour
1 teaspoon salt
½ pound white chocolate, coarsely chopped
1½ cups coarsely chopped macadamia nuts

Put the butter in a large bowl and beat until it is very soft. Gradually add both the sugars and continue beating until the mixture is light. Add the eggs, cocoa and vanilla and beat until fluffy.

Sift together the flour, baking soda and salt and fold into the butter mixture. Add the white chocolate and the nuts and mix well.

Divide the dough into 4 parts. Place each one on a large piece of aluminum foil and shape into a cylinder. Wrap the cylinders tightly in the foil and refrigerate for several hours.

Heat the oven to 350 degrees. Lightly butter 2 baking sheets.

Cut the dough cylinders into ½-inch-thick slices and put them on the baking sheets, 3 inches apart. Bake for 12 to 15 minutes, until lightly browned. Cool slightly, and then transfer the cookies to wire racks to cool completely. Slice and bake the remaining dough in the same way.

Chocolate Pecan Drops

Makes 5 dozen

Wheat germ and chopped nuts give these chocolate cookies their crunchy texture.

2 ounces unsweetened chocolate, chopped
8 tablespoons (4 ounces) butter
1⅔ cups sifted all-purpose flour
½ teaspoon baking soda
¼ teapoon salt
1 cup packed light brown sugar
⅓ cup milk
2 teaspoons vanilla extract
1 large egg
⅓ cup wheat germ
1 cup chopped pecans

Heat the oven to 350 degrees. Lightly butter 2 baking sheets.

Melt the chocolate and the butter in the top of a double boiler over hot water, stirring occasionally. Transfer the mixture to a large bowl.

Sift together the flour, baking soda and salt.

Beat the brown sugar into the chocolate mixture. Beat in the milk, vanilla and egg. Gradually add the sifted dry ingredients, alternating with the wheat germ, and beating well after each addition. Stir in the pecans.

Drop the dough onto the baking sheets in rounded teaspoonfuls, about 1 inch apart. Bake for about 10 minutes, or until the cookies spring back when lightly touched. Cool on wire racks. Bake the remaining dough in the same way.

Chocolate Banana Cookies

Makes 3 dozen

A rich, light cookie with a soft, cakey texture.

> *6 ounces semisweet chocolate, chopped*
> *2 large or 3 small very ripe bananas*
> *12 tablespoons (6 ounces) butter, softened*
> *½ cup sugar*
> *½ cup packed light brown sugar*
> *1 teaspoon vanilla extract*
> *2 large eggs*
> *2½ cups sifted all-purpose flour*
> *2 teaspoons baking powder*
> *½ teaspoon baking soda*
> *¼ teaspoon salt*
> *1 cup chopped pecans or walnuts (optional)*

Heat the oven to 400 degrees. Lightly butter 2 baking sheets.

Melt the chocolate in the top of a double boiler over hot water, stirring occasionally. Remove from the heat.

Mash the bananas to a smooth pulp.

Beat the butter until it is smooth. Beat in both the sugars and the vanilla. Add the eggs, one at a time, beating well after each addition.

Sift together the flour, baking powder, baking soda and salt. Gradually stir the dry ingredients into the butter mixture, mixing only until they are incorporated.

Add the mashed bananas and the chocolate and stir until smooth. Stir in the nuts, if you are using them.

Drop the batter onto the baking sheets in rounded teaspoonfuls, 2 inches apart. Bake for 10 to 12 minutes, or until the cookies spring back when lightly touched. Leave the cookies on the sheets for 2 to 3 minutes before transferring them to wire racks to cool. Bake the remaining batter in the same way.

It's easy to melt chocolate in the microwave oven. Put the pieces in a measuring cup and cook at Medium (50 percent power) just until the chocolate turns shiny (about 2 minutes). Remove and stir until smooth.

Chocolate Crinkles

Makes 6 dozen

These delectable cookies rise and expand as they bake, and the sugar coating on their surface crackles and crinkles.

> *4 ounces unsweetened chocolate, chopped*
> *2 cups sugar*
> *½ cup vegetable oil*
> *4 large eggs*
> *3 teaspoons vanilla extract*
> *2 cups sifted all-purpose flour*
> *2 teaspoons baking powder*
> *½ teaspoon salt*
> *Confectioners' sugar*

In a hurry? Mix the dough ahead and freeze it. Then thaw it overnight in the refrigerator, slice—and pop your cookies in the oven.

Melt the chocolate in the top of a double boiler over hot water. Remove it from the heat and stir in the sugar and the oil. Let the mixture cool slightly.

Add the eggs, one at a time, beating until the mixture is smooth. Stir in the vanilla.

Sift together the flour, baking powder and salt and stir into the chocolate mixture. The dough will be very soft. Cover and chill for several hours or overnight.

Heat the oven to 375 degrees. Lightly butter 2 baking sheets.

Break off teaspoonfuls of the dough and shape them into balls by rolling between your palms. Drop the balls into confectioners' sugar, rolling them until coated. Place the cookies on the baking sheets about 2 inches apart and bake for 8 to 12 minutes, until they are set but not browned. Be sure not to overbake—the cookies should be moist and chewy. Transfer them to wire racks to cool. Shape and bake the remaining dough in the same way.

Chocolate Stars

Makes 50

Little stars of chocolate are filled with bright dabs of fruit jam. To make them, you will need a tubular cookie press with a star tip. Cake flour, which is finer than all-purpose flour, gives them a light, crumbly texture.

2½ ounces unsweetened chocolate, chopped
1½ cups (12 ounces) butter, softened
1 cup vegetable shortening
1¾ cups sifted confectioners' sugar
6 cups sifted cake flour
3 tablespoons unsweetened cocoa powder
6 large egg whites
⅔ cup strawberry, raspberry or apricot jam or preserves

Heat the oven to 375 degrees.

Melt the chocolate in the top of a double boiler over hot water, stirring occasionally. Remove the pan from the heat and set it aside to cool slightly.

Beat the butter and shortening until they are smooth and light. Add the confectioners' sugar and beat until the mixture is fluffy. Stir in the melted chocolate.

Sift together the flour and cocoa. Add to the chocolate mixture, a quarter at a time, beating well after each addition. Beat in the egg whites.

Press the dough onto unbuttered baking sheets through a cookie press fitted with a ¾-inch star tip, leaving about 1 inch between each. Bake for about 8 minutes, until the stars are firm. Cool the cookies on wire racks. Bake the remaining dough in the same way.

When the cookies are quite cool, spread half of them with jam and top with the remaining stars. Allow to set for about an hour before serving.

Honey Oatmeal
Chocolate Drops

Makes 5 dozen

Honey is the only sweetener in these crunchy chocolate cookies.

> 2 ounces unsweetened chocolate, chopped
> 1 cup (8 ounces) butter
> 1¼ cups honey
> 2 large eggs, lightly beaten
> 1½ cups old-fashioned oatmeal
> 2½ cups sifted all-purpose flour
> 1 teaspoon baking powder
> ½ teaspoon salt
> ¼ teaspoon baking soda
> 2 teaspoons cinnamon
> 1 cup chopped pecans or shredded coconut
> 3 tablespoons wheat germ

Use regular rolled oats, sometimes known as "old-fashioned," to give the nutty, chewy texture and flavor you look for in oatmeal cookies.

Heat the oven to 325 degrees. Lightly butter 2 baking sheets.

Melt the chocolate in the top of a double boiler over hot water, stirring occasionally. Remove from the heat and set aside to cool.

Beat the butter until smooth. Add the honey and mix well. Stir in the eggs, melted chocolate and oatmeal.

Sift together the flour, baking powder, salt, baking soda and cinnamon. Gradually add the dry ingredients to the chocolate mixture, beating well after each addition. Stir in the nuts or coconut and the wheat germ.

Drop the batter onto the baking sheets in rounded teaspoonfuls and bake for 20 minutes, until the cookies are firm. Cool them on wire racks. Bake the remaining dough in the same way.

Chocolate Wafers

Makes 4 dozen

Thin, crisp and chocolaty, these wafers go splendidly with a glass of ice-cold milk.

6 ounces semisweet chocolate, chopped
8 tablespoons (4 ounces) butter, cut into pieces
⅓ cup sugar
¼ cup dark corn syrup
1 large egg, lightly beaten
1½ teaspoons vanilla extract
1 cup sifted all-purpose flour
½ teaspoon baking soda
⅛ teaspoon salt

Heat the oven to 350 degrees.

Melt the chocolate in the top of a double boiler over hot water, stirring occasionally. Remove from the heat.

Stir in the butter. Add the sugar and the corn syrup and stir until all the ingredients are melted and the mixture is smooth. Let cool for about 5 minutes.

Stir the egg briskly into the chocolate mixture. Stir in the vanilla extract.

Sift together the flour, baking soda and salt. Stir the dry ingredients into the chocolate mixture and beat until smooth.

Drop the dough onto unbuttered baking sheets in teaspoonfuls, about 2 inches apart. Bake for 8 to 12 minutes, until the cookies have risen in the oven and then fallen and flattened into wafers. Leave them on the baking sheets for 1 to 2 minutes to firm up and then transfer them to wire racks to cool. The cookies should be very crisp when completely cooled.

Bake the remaining dough in the same way.

CHAPTER 6

DESSERT COOKIES

There is no reason at all for cookies to be relegated to the realm of snacks and lunchboxes. A pretty plate of just-baked cookies makes a delicious ending to a fine meal—whether they are served as an accompaniment to a light sherbet, homemade ice cream or fresh fruit, or standing proudly on their own as dessert.

In this chapter you will find recipes developed for sophisticated tastes, from sweet nutty meringues to traditional ladyfingers. Any one of these cookies will be a welcome confection at your next dinner party.

Almond Butter Bars

Makes 4 dozen

The richness of almonds and butter makes these rectangular cookies after-dinner treats to be savored. The dough can be made in advance and stored in the refrigerator or freezer, but the cookies are best eaten the same day they are baked.

> 8 tablespoons (4 ounces) butter, softened
> ¾ cup sugar
> 2 large eggs, separated
> 1 teaspoon vanilla extract
> 1 teaspoon almond extract
> 1½ cups all-purpose flour
> ¼ teaspoon salt
> 1 teaspoon baking powder
> 1 cup ground almonds

Beat the butter and sugar until they are light and creamy. Beat in the egg yolks and the vanilla and almond extracts.

Sift together the flour, salt and baking powder. Fold the dry ingredients into the butter mixture. Cover and chill the dough for at least 1 hour.

Heat the oven to 375 degrees. Lightly butter 2 baking sheets.

Cut the dough into 4 pieces and roll it out, a piece at a time, on a lightly floured work surface to a thickness of ½ inch. Cut the dough into 1-by-2½-inch rectangles.

Beat the egg whites until they are frothy. Dip each rectangle into the whites and then roll it in the ground almonds. Put the cookies on the baking sheets and bake for 8 minutes, until the edges are lightly browned. Transfer to wire racks to cool. Bake the remaining cookies in the same way.

Ladyfingers

Makes 2 dozen

Homemade ladyfingers are crisp and delicate. They can be prepared in special molds or baked directly on lined baking sheets, as described here. When they have cooled, you can dip them into melted chocolate, make them into tempting sandwiches with flavored whipped cream or frosting, or use them to line a charlotte mold.

3 large eggs, separated
½ cup sugar
1 teaspoon vanilla extract
⅛ teaspoon salt
⅛ teaspoon cream of tartar
⅔ cup sifted cake flour
⅓ cup confectioners' sugar

For chocolate ladyfingers, use only 1/2 cup flour. Sift it with 3 tablespoons unsweetened cocoa powder and proceed with the recipe.

Heat the oven to 300 degrees. Line 2 baking sheets with kitchen parchment.

Beat the egg yolks with the sugar until they are very light in color. Stir in the vanilla.

Put the egg whites in a clean dry bowl. Add the salt and the cream of tartar and beat until soft peaks form.

Fold the egg whites and the flour alternately into the yolk mixture, a third at a time. Fold only until the ingredients are combined—do not overmix, or the ladyfingers will be too dense.

Spoon the batter into a pastry bag fitted with a ½-inch plain tip. Pipe the batter onto the lined baking sheets in 3-to-4-inch strips, leaving ½ inch between each. Bake for 20 minutes, until the ladyfingers spring back when touched lightly with your finger. Using a spatula, transfer them to wire racks to cool. Bake the remaining batter in the same way.

Sift the confectioners' sugar over the ladyfingers before serving.

Pecan Kisses

Makes 8 dozen

Lighter-than-air meringue kisses, artfully arranged on a decorative plate—who could ask for a better dessert? They will stay crisp for a day or two stored in an open container at room temperature.

4 large egg whites
⅛ teaspoon cream of tartar
½ teaspoon vanilla extract
1 cup superfine sugar
¾ cup finely chopped pecans

Heat the oven to 250 degrees. Line 2 baking sheets with foil or kitchen parchment. Butter and flour the lined sheets and shake off any excess flour.

Beat the egg whites until they are frothy. Add the cream of tartar and continue beating until soft peaks form. Gradually add the vanilla and ¾ cup of the sugar and continue beating until stiff peaks form.

Combine the remaining sugar with the chopped pecans and fold gently into the meringue.

Spoon the mixture into a pastry bag fitted with a ½-inch plain or star tip, filling the bag no more than two-thirds full. Pipe the meringue onto the baking sheets in small, round "kisses," about 1 inch apart.

Bake for 1½ hours, until the kisses are firm, dry and pale beige. Loosen them while still warm, using a metal spatula, and transfer to wire racks to cool.

Kitchen parchment is a nonabsorbent paper used when you want to seal moisture in or out of a dish. It is available in rolls in the supermarket.

Cats' Tongues

Makes 4 dozen

These are also known by their French name, *langues de chat,* and their distinctive shape is achieved by piping the cookie mixture from a pastry bag onto the baking sheets. Crispy and brown-edged, they are especially good with desserts such as sorbet, ice cream and mousse.

> *8 tablespoons (4 ounces) butter, softened*
> *½ cup sugar*
> *3 large egg whites*
> *1 teaspoon vanilla extract*
> *1 cup sifted all-purpose flour*
> *⅛ teaspoon salt*

Heat the oven to 375 degrees. Lightly butter 2 baking sheets.

Beat the butter and sugar until they are light and creamy. Add the egg whites one at a time, beating well after each addition. Stir in the vanilla and fold in the flour and salt.

Fit a pastry bag with a ½-inch plain tip. Spoon the batter into the pastry bag, no more than two-thirds full, and twist the top. Pipe the batter onto the baking sheets in 2-inch strips, leaving about 2 inches between each.

Bake in the center of the oven for 8 minutes, until the edges are lightly browned. Cool on wire racks. Bake the remaining batter in the same way.

Walnut Cookies

Makes 2½ dozen

These cookies could perhaps be called brown sugar meringues, and can be made with any kind of nut. They contain very little flour and are held together with the beaten egg whites. Do not try to hurry along the baking time by raising the oven temperature even a fraction of a degree. They need to cook very slowly and to be left in the oven after it is turned off. To keep them crisp, store them uncovered—which means they should not be kept longer than a day or two.

½ cup walnut pieces
1½ teaspoons all-purpose flour
2 large egg whites
⅛ teaspoon salt
⅛ teaspoon cream of tartar
½ teaspoon vanilla extract
¼ cup packed light brown sugar

Heat the oven to 275 degrees. Lightly butter 2 baking sheets.

Finely chop ¼ cup of the walnuts. Put the remaining nuts in a food processor or blender. Add the flour and process until the nuts are ground. Do not overgrind.

Put the egg whites in a bowl. Add the salt and cream of tartar and beat until soft peaks form. Add the vanilla and then the sugar, 1 tablespoon at a time, and continue beating until stiff peaks form. Fold in the ground and chopped walnuts.

Drop the mixture onto the baking sheets in teaspoonfuls and bake for 1 hour. Turn off the oven but do not open the door. Leave the cookies in the oven for 1 hour longer. They will be crisp on the outside and chewy inside.

Almond Crescents

Makes 2 1/2 dozen

These fragile crescent cookies are so buttery and nutty that they crumble in your mouth. They are easy to make if the dough is thoroughly chilled—and even easier if you mix the dough in a food processor.

12 tablespoons (6 ounces) butter, softened
1 cup confectioners' sugar
2 cups sifted flour
¾ cup ground almonds
1 teaspoon almond extract

If you have a food processor, grinding nuts is easy—but don't overgrind, or you will have nut paste!

Beat the butter with ¼ cup of the confectioners' sugar until the mixture is light and creamy. Fold in the flour, ground almonds and almond extract. Alternatively, put all the ingredients in a food processor and process for 2 seconds at a time, using the pulse control, until a smooth dough forms. Pat the dough into a ball, wrap in transparent wrap and chill for at least 1 hour, until firm.

Heat the oven to 325 degrees. Lightly butter 2 baking sheets.

Pinch off a teaspoon of dough at a time and roll it between your palms to form a small cylinder. Bend the cylinders into crescents and put them on the baking sheets. Bake for 10 minutes, then transfer the cookies to wire racks to cool. Bake the remaining dough in the same way.

When the cookies are cool enough to handle, dredge them with the remaining ¾ cup confectioners' sugar.

Lemon Bars

Makes 2 dozen

These tangy-sweet little squares are always popular—
and easy to make, too.

> 8 tablespoons (4 ounces) butter, softened
> ¼ cup confectioners' sugar
> 1 cup plus 2 tablespoons all-purpose flour
> 1 cup sugar
> ½ teaspoon baking powder
> 2 large eggs
> 3 tablespoons lemon juice
> 2 teaspoons grated lemon rind

Heat the oven to 350 degrees. Butter an 8-inch-
square baking pan.

Cream the butter with the confectioners' sugar for 2
to 3 minutes, until fluffy. Stir in 1 cup of flour. Press
the mixture evenly into the pan and bake for 15 minutes. Remove the pan from the oven and let cool
slightly. Do not turn off the oven.

Combine the granulated sugar with the remaining
flour, the baking powder and the eggs and beat until
smooth. Stir in the lemon juice and rind. Pour the
mixture over the baked crust and return the pan to the
oven for 25 minutes. Cool to room temperature before
cutting into bars.

To take advantage
of the natural oil
in the skin, always
grate citrus rind
from fresh fruits.

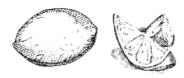

Coconut Meringue Drops

Makes 3 dozen

Sweetened coconut is one of the most pleasing ingredients to combine with meringue. Remember to make these on a dry day so that they will be light and crispy.

>   2 large egg whites
>   ⅛ teaspoon salt
>   ⅛ teaspoon cream of tartar
>   ½ teaspoon vanilla extract
>   ½ cup sugar
>   ¼ cup all-purpose flour
>   ¾ cup sweetened flaked coconut

Heat the oven to 200 degrees. Lightly butter 2 baking sheets.

Put the egg whites, salt and cream of tartar in a large bowl and beat at high speed until soft peaks form. Add the sugar, 1 tablespoon at a time, and continue beating until the whites are stiff and shiny. Fold in the flour and coconut.

Drop the meringue onto the baking sheets in teaspoonfuls and bake for 1 hour. Turn the oven off and leave the meringues in the oven, with the door shut, for 1 hour longer.

CHAPTER 7

BROWNIES AND BARS

Everyone loves a good brownie. Some people prefer their brownies dense and moist, others like them cakey and light. Whatever your preference, you will find a brownie or bar cookie perfectly suited to your taste in this chapter. And besides having wonderful flavor and texture, brownies and bars are simple to make. In most recipes, you do not even need an electric mixer. It takes only minutes to stir the ingredients together by hand.

Brownies and bars are just right for afternoon snacks and brown-bag fare; they are equally good as dessert. Have you tried dark chocolaty brownies and fresh raspberries, or a butterscotch bar topped with buttercrunch ice cream and maple sauce? Set a plate of brownies or bars on the table at your next club meeting or family party. The plate will be empty before you know it—so be sure to squirrel away a square or two in the kitchen for yourself.

Hollywood Brownies

Makes 1 ½ dozen

Brownies with such an intense chocolate flavor deserve an award for best performance.

5 ounces unsweetened chocolate, chopped
11 tablespoons (5½ ounces) butter
4 large eggs
2 teaspoons vanilla extract
1 cup sugar
1 cup packed light brown sugar
2 teaspoons baking powder
2 cups sifted all-purpose flour
1 teaspoon salt
1 cup chopped walnuts

Heat the oven to 350 degrees. Butter a 9–inch–square baking pan.

Combine the chocolate with the butter in the top of a double boiler over hot water. Stir until the chocolate melts and the mixture is smooth.

Beat the eggs until they are pale yellow. Add the vanilla and both the sugars and mix until blended. Stir in the melted chocolate.

Sift together the dry ingredients and gradually stir them into the chocolate mixture. Fold in the nuts and spread the batter in the prepared pan.

Bake for 45 to 50 minutes, until a toothpick inserted in the center comes out clean. Cool the brownies, still in the pan, on a wire rack. When cool, cut into squares.

Almond Brownies

Makes 3 dozen

Rolled oats give these brownies a pleasantly chewy texture and the almonds add a subtle flavor that blends well with the cocoa.

½ cup unsweetened cocoa powder
11 tablespoons (5½ ounces) butter, melted
1 cup packed light brown sugar
⅓ cup honey
½ teaspoon salt
½ teaspoon almond extract
1 cup slivered almonds
4 cups rolled oats

Heat the oven to 350 degrees. Line a 10-by-15-inch pan with wax paper or aluminum foil, leaving an overhang of about 1 inch at each end. Butter and lightly flour the paper.

Stir the cocoa into the melted butter while it is still warm. Fold in the remaining ingredients, one at a time, stirring until just combined.

Spread the batter in the prepared pan and bake for 25 to 30 minutes. Using the overhanging paper as handles, lift the brownies out of the pan and cool on wire racks before cutting into squares.

STORING BAR COOKIES

If the bars will be eaten soon after baking, simply leave them in the pan and cover it with foil. If you plan to store them for more than a day or two, take them out of the pan and wrap them in foil. Bar cookies freeze well, wrapped in a double thickness of foil. Let them thaw at room temperature.

Apricot and Date Bars

Makes 16

The sweet, dense flavors of dried apricots and dates are heightened by just a touch of port.

> *½ cup chopped dried dates*
> *½ cup chopped dried apricots*
> *3 large eggs*
> *¾ cup sugar*
> *1 tablespoon port wine*
> *1 cup chopped walnuts or pecans*
> *¼ cup matzoh meal*

Pour enough boiling water over the dates and apricots to cover them. Let them stand for 15 minutes. Drain in a colander.

Heat the oven to 325 degrees. Butter an 8-inch-square pan and dust it lightly with flour or matzoh meal, shaking out the excess.

Beat the eggs until they are pale yellow. Stir in the sugar and the port. Add the drained fruit and the nuts. Stir in the matzoh meal.

Spoon the mixture into the pan and bake for 45 to 50 minutes. Cool the cake in the pan before cutting into bars.

Butterscotch Toffee Bars

Makes 4 dozen

Nothing beats the richness of butterscotch.

> *1 cup (8 ounces) butter, softened*
> *1 cup packed dark brown sugar*

2 large egg yolks
2 cups all-purpose flour
½ teaspoon salt
1½ teaspoons cinnamon
1 egg white, lightly beaten
¼ cup chopped walnuts
½ cup butterscotch morsels

Heat the oven to 350 degrees. Butter a 10-by-15-inch baking pan.

Beat the butter with the sugar until the mixture is pale and fluffy. Stir in the egg yolks.

Sift together the flour, salt and cinnamon and stir them into the butter mixture.

Press the dough into the prepared pan. Brush the surface with the egg white and sprinkle with the nuts and butterscotch morsels.

Bake for 25 minutes, until firm in the center. Cut into bars while still warm.

MAILING COOKIES

Brownies and bars are among the best cookies for mailing. Even so, they should be treated with great care. Large soft cookies and drop cookies are also good candidates. Crisp cookies tend to become crumbs when entrusted to the post office. Follow these instructions for mailing all cookies.

Wrap the bars or cookies separately and pack them closely in a metal tin so that they will not move about. (You can use marshmallows to fill in any small spaces.) Line a heavy cardboard box with shredded newspaper or styrofoam pellets and settle the tin on this padding. Pile more packing material on top so that the tin is securely wedged in its midst. Tape the box well, wrap it in brown paper and write, in large, bold letters: PERISHABLE, HANDLE WITH CARE.

Send by first class or air parcel post. Someone out there will thank you for your care!

Chocolate Chip Brownies

Makes 1 dozen

A winning combination of two of America's favorites—chocolate chip cookies and brownies.

2½ cups semisweet chocolate morsels
¾ cup sugar
6 tablespoons (3 ounces) butter
1 teaspoon vanilla extract
2 tablespoons milk
2 large eggs
¾ cup flour
½ teaspoon baking soda
½ teaspoon salt

Heat the oven to 325 degrees. Butter an 8-inch-square baking pan.

Combine half the chocolate morsels with the sugar, butter, vanilla and milk in a small saucepan. Stir over low heat until the chocolate and butter are melted and the mixture is smooth. Remove from the heat and cool slightly. Add the eggs and beat well.

Sift together the dry ingredients and add them to the chocolate mixture, stirring well to combine. Stir in the remaining chocolate morsels.

Spread the batter evenly in the pan and bake for 30 to 35 minutes. Cool the brownies in the pan and then cut them into 12 squares.

Chess Bars

Makes 2 dozen

Chess pie is an old American favorite—a sweet, sticky brown sugar pie. These bars are a most satisfactory variation on the theme.

1 cup (8 ounces) butter, melted
2 cups packed light brown sugar
1 cup sugar
4 large eggs
2 cups all-purpose flour
½ teaspoon salt
2 teaspoons baking powder
Confectioners' sugar, for dusting

Heat the oven to 300 degrees. Butter a 9-by-13-inch pan and dust lightly with flour.

Combine the butter and both the sugars in a large bowl and stir until smooth. Add the eggs, one at a time, beating well after each addition.

Sift together the flour, salt and baking powder and stir into the butter mixture.

Pour the batter into the pan and bake for 1 hour, until a toothpick inserted in the center comes out clean. Let the cake cool in the pan, then dust it with confectioners' sugar and cut into bars.

Peanut Butter Brownies

Makes 2 dozen

For the crunchiest, nuttiest brownies in town, make these with chunky peanut butter. Creamy is just as tasty, though.

> *3 large eggs*
> *1 cup packed light brown sugar*
> *½ cup sugar*
> *½ cup peanut butter*
> *1 teaspoon vanilla extract*
> *2 tablespoons butter, softened*
> *½ cup cake flour*
> *1 teaspoon baking powder*
> *1 teaspoon salt*
> *½ cup salted chopped peanuts*

Heat the oven to 350 degrees. Butter a 9-inch-square cake pan.

Beat the eggs with both sugars, peanut butter, vanilla extract and butter until smooth.

Sift together the flour, baking powder and salt and stir them into the egg mixture.

Spread the batter evenly in the pan and sprinkle the peanuts over the surface. Bake for 30 minutes. Let the brownies cool in the pan for 10 to 15 minutes and cut them into 24 bars while still warm.

CHAPTER 8

TRADITIONAL AND HOLIDAY COOKIES

Holidays, particularly those around Christmas, are cookie-baking times. Cooks who at other seasons of the year bake only bread or an occasional cake, butter up the baking sheets and begin mixing cookie dough. Rolling pins are pulled from the back of kitchen drawers and cookie cutters are polished up for their annual workout. Supermarket shelves overflow with nuts, chocolate, colored sugars, candy decorations and decorating tools, as well as extra stocks of flour, sugar, spices and eggs. It seems, suddenly, as if everyone is baking.

Many of the cookie recipes in this chapter reflect a national heritage, and one of the pleasures of the American melting pot is that we are free to adopt the recipes of many other lands, or set up new traditions of our own. But whether holiday cookies evoke memories of faraway countries or of past family celebrations, they always add their own unique dimension to current good times.

Pfeffernusse

Makes 4 dozen

If you prefer, you can make these traditional German Christmas cookies with vegetable shortening instead of butter. They are a little easier to handle when made with butter, but the end result in both cases is deliciously crumbly and marvelously spicy.

8 tablespoons (4 ounces) butter, softened
1 cup sugar
2½ cups sifted all-purpose flour
½ teaspoon salt
1 teaspoon cinnamon
½ teaspoon powdered ginger
½ teaspoon ground nutmeg
¼ teaspoon white pepper
2 large eggs, beaten
¼ cup ground almonds
¼ cup rum
½ cup confectioners' sugar

Beat the butter and sugar in a large bowl until the mixture is light and creamy.

Sift together the flour, salt, spices and pepper.

Add ½ cup of the dry ingredients to the butter mixture. Stir in half the beaten eggs and mix thoroughly. Stir in the remaining dry ingredients and beaten egg. Add the almonds and stir gently until thoroughly combined. Cover and chill the batter for at least 2 hours.

Heat the oven to 375 degrees. Lightly butter 2 baking sheets.

Pinch off small pieces of the chilled dough and form them into ½-inch balls. Put them on the baking sheets and bake for 10 minutes.

Let the cookies cool on the sheets for 10 to 15 min-

Store the cookies in an airtight container in the refrigerator. If you can keep from eating them for a week you will be rewarded by an even spicier cookie.

utes and then sprinkle them with the rum. While the cookies are still slightly warm, roll them in confectioners' sugar. Let them cool completely, before storing in an airtight container.

Scottish Shortbread

Makes 20 pieces

Luckily for those of us who find shortbread simply splendid, it is easy to bake at home, both for year-round enjoyment and Christmas giving.

1 cup (8 ounces) butter, softened
½ cup plus 2 tablespoons sugar
2 cups sifted all-purpose flour
¼ teaspoon salt
¼ teaspoon baking powder

Heat the oven to 350 degrees.

Beat the butter until it is light and creamy. Add ½ cup of the sugar and beat until the mixture is fluffy.

Sift the flour with the salt and the baking powder and fold into the butter mixture.

Put the dough on an unbuttered baking sheet and pat it into a ½-inch-thick rectangle. Mark the dough into 1-by-2-inch bars with the point of a knife. Sprinkle with the remaining sugar and bake in the center of the oven for 15 minutes, until the edges are very lightly browned.

Cool the shortbread on the baking sheet for 15 minutes and then cut into bars as marked.

Holiday Pretzels

Makes 4 dozen

These cookies are twisted into pretzel shapes and then are "salted" with a mixture of sugar and cinnamon.

1 cup (8 ounces) butter, softened
½ cup sour cream
1 large egg yolk
2½ cups sifted all-purpose flour
½ teaspoon salt
1 cup sugar
½ cup pearl or decorating sugar
1 teaspoon cinnamon
1 large egg, beaten

These cookies are fun to make, especially if you have kids around to roll the dough into strands.

Beat the butter until it is fluffy. Stir in the sour cream and the egg yolk.

Sift together the flour, salt and sugar. Stir the dry ingredients gradually into the butter mixture to make a soft dough. Chill for 30 minutes, or until firm enough to handle.

Divide the dough into 4 pieces and roll them with the flat of your hands into ropes about 12 inches long. Wrap the ropes in transparent wrap and chill for at least 1 hour more.

Heat the oven to 350 degrees. Lightly butter 2 baking sheets.

Cut each rope of dough into 12 pieces. Roll each piece into a strand about 4 inches long and ⅛ inch thick. Twist each strand into a pretzel shape and place on the baking sheets about ½ inch apart.

Stir together the pearl sugar and cinnamon. Brush the pretzels with the beaten egg and sprinkle them with the cinnamon sugar. Bake for 20 minutes, until crisp and lightly browned. Cool on wire racks. Repeat with the remaining dough.

Kourabiedes

Makes 8 dozen

Rich, buttery and infused with a delicate flavor of cloves, these cookies are a time-honored part of Greek Easter celebrations. Baked cloves have a far milder flavor than uncooked ones and you will find they also add a pleasant crunchiness.

1 cup (8 ounces) butter, softened
⅓ cup sugar
2 large egg yolks
2 teaspoons vanilla extract
½ teaspoon brandy (optional)
2 cups all-purpose flour
1 teaspoon baking powder
⅛ teaspoon salt
Cloves

Beat the butter until it is light and smooth. Add the sugar, egg yolks, vanilla and brandy and mix well.

Sift together the flour, baking powder and salt and stir gradually into the butter mixture until the dough forms a ball. Cover and chill for 1 hour.

Heat the oven to 350 degrees. Lightly butter 2 baking sheets.

Pinch off teaspoon-sized pieces of dough and roll them into egg shapes or balls between your palms. Place them on the baking sheets and insert a clove into the top of each cookie. Bake for 10 to 12 minutes, until the cookies are firm but not browned. Remove them from the oven, cool on the baking sheets for 1 to 2 minutes and transfer to wire racks to cool completely. Repeat with the remaining dough.

Lebkuchen

Makes 5 dozen

These traditional Christmas cookies from Germany
will taste even better if you chill the dough for up to
three days before baking.

> ¾ *cup honey*
> ¾ *cup firmly packed dark brown sugar*
> *2 tablespoons (1 ounce) butter*
> *1 large egg*
> *Grated rind of 1 orange*
> *3½ cups sifted all-purpose flour*
> *½ teaspoon salt*
> *½ teaspoon baking soda*
> *1 teaspoon cinnamon*
> *1 teaspoon allspice*
> *½ teaspoon ground nutmeg*
> *½ teaspoon powdered ginger*
> ¾ *cup finely chopped glacéed fruits*
> ¾ *cup slivered almonds, finely chopped*

> GLAZE:
> *1 cup confectioners' sugar*
> *3–4 tablespoons water*

Store the cookies
in an airtight tin
for weeks to allow
their full flavor to
develop.

Pour the honey into a saucepan. Add the sugar and
the butter and stir over moderate heat until the sugar
dissolves and the butter melts. Do not let the honey
boil. Let the mixture cool to room temperature.

Stir in the egg and the orange rind.

Sift together the flour, salt, baking soda and spices
and fold into the honey mixture. Stir in the glacéed
fruit and almonds. Cover the dough and chill overnight.

Heat the oven to 350 degrees. Lightly butter 2 baking
sheets.

Divide the dough into 4 pieces and roll each out on

a lightly floured work surface into a 6-by-5-inch rectangle, ¾ inch thick. Cut the dough into 1-by-2½-inch bars, set them on the prepared sheets and bake for 10 minutes. Transfer the cookies to wire racks.

To make the glaze, combine the confectioners' sugar with 3 tablespoons of water and stir to blend. If it is too stiff, add more water by the teaspoonful until it reaches the right consistency for a thin coating. Brush or spread the glaze on the cookies while they are still warm.

Let the lebkuchen cool completely before storing.

Spritz Cookies

Makes 3 dozen

> 8 tablespoons (4 ounces) butter, softened
> ¼ cup sugar
> 2 large egg whites
> 1 teaspoon vanilla extract
> 1¼ cups sifted all-purpose flour
> ⅛ teaspoon salt

Beat the butter and sugar until they are light and creamy. Stir in the egg whites and the vanilla. Fold in the flour and the salt and chill the dough for at least 1 hour.

Heat the oven to 375 degrees. Lightly butter 2 baking sheets.

Spoon the dough into a cookie press and press out the various shapes you fancy, using the interchangeable plates. Alternatively, roll the dough out on a lightly floured work surface and cut it into shapes with a roller cutter that has several designs on it.

Bake the cookies for 8 minutes, until the edges are very lightly browned. Cool them on wire racks. Decorate while they are still slightly warm.

Spritz cookies (*spritz* means press or squirt in German) are shaped in a cookie press—a cylinder-shaped gadget through which you press the dough. Vary colors as well as shapes by tinting with food colorings.

Gingerbread Folk

Makes 2 dozen

These deliciously gingery little people make great Christmas tree decorations. Pierce a small hole in the top of each unbaked cookie with a wooden toothpick and leave the toothpicks in place during baking. When the cookies have cooled, remove the toothpicks and pull lengths of red or green thread or fine ribbon through the holes.

12 tablespoons (6 ounces) butter, softened
½ cup firmly packed brown sugar
1 large egg
¾ cup molasses
3 cups sifted all-purpose flour
¼ teaspoon salt
2 teaspoons powdered ginger
1 teaspoon cinnamon
½ teaspoon ground cloves
½ teaspoon ground nutmeg

Gingerbread folk are fun to decorate. Use raisins, nuts, gumdrops, colored sugar, candied fruit, white or colored frosting— anything, in fact, that looks and tastes good.

Beat the butter with the sugar until the mixture is light and creamy. Stir in the egg and the molasses.

Sift together the remaining ingredients and fold them into the butter mixture. Cover and chill the dough for 2 hours.

Heat the oven to 375 degrees. Lightly butter 2 baking sheets.

Divide the chilled dough into 4 pieces. Roll each piece out on a floured work surface with a lightly floured rolling pin to a thickness of about ¼ inch. Stamp out the dough with cookie cutters and place the cookies on the baking sheets. Bake for 10 to 12 minutes and cool the cookies on wire racks.

Repeat the process until all the dough is used up.

INDEX